P9-BJM-200

LOLLIPOP LOVE

LOLLIPOP LOVE

Sweet Indulgence with Chocolate, Caramel, and Sugar

Anita Chu

PHOTOGRAPHS BY ANTONIS ACHILLEOS

CHRONICLE BOOKS

SAN FRANCISCO

To Mike and Isabelle, the sweetest parts of my life.

TEXT COPYRIGHT © 2015 BY ANITA CHU.
PHOTOGRAPHS COPYRIGHT © 2015 BY ANTONIS ACHILLEOS.

LIBRARY OF CONGRESS CATALOGING-IN-PUBLICATION DATA:

Chu, Anita.

Lollipop love : sweet indulgence with chocolate, caramel, and sugar /

   Anita Chu ; photographs by Antonis Achilleos.

    pages cm

  Includes index.

  ISBN-13 978-1-4521-2593-0 — ISBN-10 1-4521-2593-7 1. Lollipops. I. Title.

  TX791.C5593 2015

  641.85'3—dc23

                       2014015022

MANUFACTURED IN CHINA

DESIGNED AND ILLUSTRATED BY AZI RAD
PROP STYLING BY CATHY COOK
FOOD STYLING BY CATHY COOK
TYPESETTING BY DC TYPE

Pop Rocks is a registered trademark of
Pop Rocks, Inc.

10 9 8 7 6 5 4 3 2 1

Chronicle Books LLC
680 Second Street
San Francisco, California 94107
WWW.CHRONICLEBOOKS.COM

CONTENTS

INTRODUCTION

Lollipops are the original sweet on a stick, the quintessential candy of childhood. I remember the brightly colored, cellophane-wrapped pops from the dentist's office, the giant rainbow-swirled lollipops at the carnival, the round suckers with a chewy center that took a whole afternoon to finish. Today, lollipops are no longer just child's candy but a grown-up sweet. You can find them in flavors like espresso-rum and mango-chili, made with beer or champagne, and decorated with glitter dust, cacao nibs, and rose petals.

The history behind lollipops is delightfully colorful. In late-eighteenth-century England, street vendors sold sugar candy and called them lolly pops, *lolly* being slang at the time for "tongue" or "mouth." The name could thus be interpreted as a sweet you could pop in your mouth. Although some sources claim that certain vendors did put their wares on sticks to make them easier for children to eat, in general, the term *lolly pop* did not mean candy on a stick. The words *lolly pop*, *lollypop*, and *lollipop* can be found in various dictionaries and publications from the time period, and even in some of Charles Dickens's novels.

Fast-forward to America in the early 1900s and enterprising businessmen were inventing machines that could automate many manufacturing processes, including candy making. Several companies lay claim to being the first to put sticks into their candies, although none of them called their products "lollipops." Finally, the Bradley Smith Company brought the candy-on-a-stick concept and the words *lolly pop* together when one of the owners, George Smith, trademarked the term in 1931 to specifically describe his sugar candies on a stick. Company lore states that Smith took the name from his favorite racehorse, Lolly Pop, and not the old British term. Whether he was aware of the history behind the phrase *lolly pop*, or it was just a fantastic coincidence, is an unanswered question.

Sadly for the Bradley Smith Company, it went out of business during the Great Depression and the trademark ran out, freeing it up to be used for an endless variety of candies stuck on a stick. Today, lollipops in all shapes and flavors can be found, ranging from traditional hard sugar to caramels. When most people hear the word *lollipop*, though, they still think of a hard sugar candy perched on a stick.

Candy making might seem intimidating, since it requires thermometers and molds and involves sugar being cooked to bubbling hot temperatures, but in reality lollipops are some of the easiest candies to make. The ingredients for a simple lollipop can be found in nearly anyone's cupboard, and even without lollipop molds you can still make some pretty pops.

Once you start delving into the wide world of different molds and decorations, you can start really making your lollipops unique. Thanks to the Internet, there are molds available for nearly every occasion or theme you can imagine. Many of the decorations used in baking, such as edible glitter and sprinkles, can be used to decorate lollipops as well. Lollipops can be quickly made for an unexpected after-school treat or can be fancied up to serve as party favors.

In this book, you'll find recipes for a variety of lollipops, from traditional clear sugar pops to ones made from caramel or chocolate. There are classic dime-store flavors like super lemon and red hot, and modern flavors like maple-bacon-walnut and passion fruit–caramel. Old-fashioned styles of lollipop, like barley sugar pops and rock candy, are also included, as well as lollipops with newer ingredients, like agave syrup and Pop Rocks. Once you start making lollipops, you'll realize that the possibilities are endless. It's time to get sweet!

INGREDIENTS

CHOCOLATE
Most baking chocolates can be used for the recipes in this book. Higher-quality chocolate brands, especially ones marketed to professionals, will likely melt and temper more easily, but it's not necessary to buy the most expensive chocolate; simply use one that you enjoy. Two of my favorite brands are Guittard and Scharffen Berger, both relatively affordable chocolates that are widely available and perform well in baking and candy making. Be sure to use pure chocolate and not chocolate chips or chocolate candy bars, as they contain additional ingredients that will prevent them from tempering properly.

COLORINGS
Liquid (water-based) and gel paste food colorings both blend well into lollipops, although gel colorings will give you the most intense results because they are more concentrated.

CORN SYRUP
Corn syrup is mainly used in candy making to help prevent crystallization. Use light corn syrup to avoid adding color to your lollipops. (Note that "light" refers to the color, not "lite" as in low-calorie. The most common forms of corn syrup you'll find at the grocery store are light and dark.)

DECORATIONS
Using edible glitter, disco dust, or another edible decorating dust is one of the easiest ways to decorate your lollipops. You can swirl some into the sugar syrup before you pour it out or you can fill half the lollipop

mold with sugar syrup, sprinkle some glitter over the lollipops, and then fill up the rest of the mold to create a beautiful sparkling layer within the lollipops.

Other traditional edible decorations made of sugar—such as sprinkles, dragées, or sparkling sugars—can also be used to decorate lollipops, but as they might melt or get stuck in a candy funnel if you're using one, they are better sprinkled over the tops of lollipops after they've been poured and before they've fully set.

FLAVORINGS

Most of the recipes in this book rely on natural ingredients to add flavor to the lollipops. However, the more traditional approach is to use candy flavoring oils. These highly concentrated oils work well in lollipops because water- or alcohol-based extracts will evaporate in the high heat of the cooking sugar. Candy flavoring oils are more concentrated than extracts, meaning you'll get stronger results with less product. If you'd like to experiment with some more fanciful flavors like marshmallow or cotton candy, these oils are an easy option. The wide range of flavors available (see Resources, page 93) means you can make a huge variety of lollipops simply by adding different flavors to the sugar syrup. Some flavors work better than others depending on the brand and your personal taste.

SUGAR

Granulated sugar is the base of the classic lollipop. It doesn't matter what brand you use, but make sure it's fresh and free of any impurities.

TECHNIQUES

WORKING WITH SUGAR

Much of candy making involves boiling sugar and water together to high temperatures, forming a sugar syrup. At different temperatures, the syrup will cool to a different hardness and consistency. It's important to be able to determine exactly what stage the sugar has reached; otherwise, your candies may not set up properly. To check the temperature of cooking sugar, you can use a candy thermometer or the cold-water test.

A candy thermometer is the quickest and most accurate way to check your sugar syrup. (See page 23 for tips on selecting a candy thermometer). Be sure the bulb of the thermometer is fully immersed in the sugar syrup to ensure a correct reading.

The cold-water test is the original, classic method for checking cooking sugar and was devised in the seventeenth century, before home thermometers were generally available. The method is still used today, but it does require a bit of skill and experience on the candy maker's part to recognize the different stages. However, it can be a fun exercise to help you recognize the different stages of sugar.

The cold-water test involves taking a small amount of the hot sugar syrup and dropping it into a bowl of cold water. This will immediately halt the cooking of the sugar. Then the form of the cooled sugar is observed; from this, the stage of the sugar is determined.

The names of the stages of boiling sugar are based on the various forms the cooled sugar takes in the cold-water test. They are listed on page 13, along with the temperature ranges and typical candies that are made from sugar at that particular stage.

Candy Making Temperature Guide

TEMPERATURE	STAGE	TYPICAL USES
223°F TO 235°F **106°C TO 113°C**	THREAD	
235°F TO 240°F **113°C TO 116°C**	SOFT BALL	FUDGE, FONDANT
245°F TO 250°F **118°C TO 121°C**	FIRM BALL	CARAMELS
250°F TO 265°F **121°C TO 129°C**	HARD BALL	NOUGAT, MARSHMALLOWS
270°F TO 290°F **132°C TO 143°C**	SOFT CRACK	TAFFY, BUTTERSCOTCH
300°F TO 310°F **149°C TO 154°C**	HARD CRACK	LOLLIPOPS, BRITTLE
320°F AND ABOVE **160°C AND ABOVE**	CARAMEL	

Descriptions of each stage

Thread: Sugar will stretch into thin threads in cold water.

Soft Ball: Sugar will form into a ball in cold water but will lose its shape when taken out.

Firm Ball: Sugar will form into a ball in cold water and keep its form when taken out but will flatten easily when pressed.

Hard Ball: Sugar will form into a ball in cold water and keep its form when taken out. It is still slightly malleable but not easily flattened.

Soft Crack: Sugar will form into long threads in cold water. The threads will be stretchy and flexible when taken out.

Hard Crack: Sugar will form into long threads in cold water. The threads will be brittle and snap easily when taken out.

Caramel: Sugar will start turning golden yellow. If it is allowed to continue cooking, eventually it will burn and turn black. Be careful once the sugar reaches 300°F/149°C because it can burn in seconds.

What Is Crystallization?

Crystallization occurs when a stray sugar crystal or particle gets into the sugar syrup, making the dissolved sugar turn back into solid form. The entire mixture may eventually turn into a crackly, solid mass, and you will need to throw it away and start again with a clean saucepan. Agitating the syrup at the wrong time can also cause crystallization.

To avoid crystallization be vigilant when cooking sugar to avoid getting any undissolved sugar crystals into the mixture. Another common method is to add an ingredient to the mixture that helps prevent crystallization. These ingredients are called interfering agents.

Interfering agents used in candy making include acids, such as cream of tartar or lemon juice; glucose, such as corn syrup; and fats, such as butter or cream. They work by preventing the sucrose molecules in the dissolved sugar from sticking back together and forming a big clump of sugar crystals. Acids work by breaking the sucrose molecules into glucose and fructose molecules, which do not crystallize. Glucose and fat both work by blocking the sucrose molecules from sticking together and crystallizing. Light corn syrup is the most common interfering agent used because it is very effective and does not impart any additional color or flavor.

Alternatives to Corn Syrup

Although some people have concerns about the health effects of consuming too much corn syrup, note that in general the warnings you read are about high-fructose corn syrup. The corn syrup found at most grocery stores and that is specified for the recipes in this book is not high-fructose. It is regular corn syrup, which is mostly glucose. The high glucose content is what makes corn syrup so effective at preventing crystallization, and why most candy recipes that require cooking sugar call for it. When looking for substitutes, keep in mind that you are looking for high glucose content. Common substitutes such as honey, golden syrup, or agave nectar have a lower glucose content and more fructose, so the resulting candies may not set up as hard or will soften very quickly.

One easy substitute you can make at home is invert sugar. The process adds an acid like lemon juice or cream of tartar to sugar. The acid acts as an interfering agent and "inverts" the sugar, breaking it down into its fructose and glucose components, which will not crystallize.

INVERT SUGAR

3 cups/600 g sugar

1½ cups/360 ml water

¼ tsp lemon juice or cream of tartar

Combine the sugar, water, and lemon juice in a heavy saucepan and bring to a boil over medium heat, stirring until the sugar is dissolved. If any sugar crystals get on the sides of the saucepan, use a wet pastry brush to wash them back into the mixture. Continue cooking without stirring until it reaches 235°F/113°C and then remove from the heat and let cool. Store in an airtight container in the refrigerator for up to 6 months. You can make a one-for-one substitution for corn syrup.

CAUTION: WORKING WITH HOT SUGAR

Always exercise caution when cooking sugar. The mixture can reach extremely high temperatures and can cause serious burns if it gets on your skin. Never touch the cooking sugar mixture with your bare hands. When pouring out the hot sugar syrup, wear oven mitts to protect your hands. If you have children or pets, be sure they are supervised and will not distract or surprise you.

If you do get hot sugar on yourself, immerse the burned area under cool running water or in a bowl of cool water for 15 to 20 minutes until the pain and redness have lessened. Don't put ice directly on the area because the extreme cold could worsen the damage. Apply some burn cream or aloe vera gel to the area afterward and wrap with sterile gauze to help protect it. Of course, if the burn is more serious, you feel unwell, or it does not heal in a few days, do get medical attention.

CLEANING OUT HARDENED SUGAR IN A POT

The easiest way to remove hardened sugar that will cause the least damage to you and your equipment is to fill the pot with water, place it on the stove, and let the water come to a boil. The hot water will soften the hardened caramel, and it should come off with a minimum of scrubbing. Any other hard-caramel-covered tools can be cleaned similarly by soaking in very hot water or placing under running hot water until the sugar melts away.

WORKING WITH CHOCOLATE

Melting Chocolate

Chocolate burns easily, so it should be melted with care. The best way to melt chocolate is in a double boiler or in a metal bowl placed over a saucepan of simmering water. The water in the double boiler or saucepan should be just simmering but not boiling. The bottom of the bowl holding the chocolate should not touch the water directly, as this can also cause the chocolate to burn.

Chop the chocolate into small pieces so they will melt quickly and evenly. Sometimes you can find chocolate sold in individual wafers or discs (these are not the same as chocolate chips) that are made to melt quickly, eliminating the need for chopping. Stir often and gently with a rubber spatula to help the chocolate melt evenly and to prevent burning.

Avoid getting water or any liquids into melted chocolate, as it can make the chocolate seize. When this happens, the cocoa particles in the chocolate clump around the liquid, turning the mixture into a grainy, unusable mass. To avoid this, make sure your tools are dry.

MOISTURE AND LOLLIPOP MAKING DON'T MIX

When making any candy that involves cooking sugar, it's best to do it on a clear, dry day. Humidity adversely affects candies; because sugar absorbs water, any excess moisture in the air may lengthen the cooking process, or the cooking sugar may never reach the right stage or set up properly. This is also why candy that is left out uncovered will eventually absorb moisture from the air and become soft and sticky. If it's raining or very humid, try to put off your lollipop making for another day, or if your kitchen has air-conditioning, make it as cool and dry as possible. Also, store all finished lollipops in an airtight container or individually sealed plastic bags in a cool, dry place away from sunlight and moisture.

You can also melt dark chocolate in the microwave. Place the chocolate, finely chopped, in a heatproof bowl and heat on 50 percent of maximum power in 10-second increments, stirring thoroughly after each interval. If you use the microwave, be careful and watch the chocolate closely to avoid burning. Milk and white chocolates are more delicate than dark chocolate, so it is safer to melt them using the double boiler method instead.

Tempering Chocolate

Tempering chocolate is the process of melting chocolate, cooling it, and then heating it to the right temperature so that when it finally cools and sets, it will achieve a glossy shine and appealing hardness. Untempered chocolate that has cooled and set appears dull and streaky, feels rough, and has an unappealing chewy texture.

A few general guidelines before tempering:

- Use good-quality baking chocolate; it will make the tempering process go more smoothly. Brands like Guittard and Scharffen Berger work well.

- You'll often find baking chocolate in bars or blocks. Chop them up into small pieces so they will melt faster and more evenly. Chocolate in individual discs doesn't need to be chopped.

- Use at least 1½ to 2 lb/680 to 910 g of chocolate for tempering. With smaller amounts, it becomes difficult to control the temperature changes, and it will likely cool down and set too quickly. Some of the recipes in this book call for amounts of tempered chocolate smaller than 1½ lb/680 g. In that case, you should still temper a minimum of 1½ lb/680 g of chocolate. Any

chocolate left over after you make the recipe can be poured out onto a piece of parchment paper. After it solidifies, you can either melt and retemper it when you need more tempered chocolate or simply use it in another recipe.

QUICK/SEED METHOD FOR TEMPERING CHOCOLATE:

1. Finely chop 1½ to 2 lb/680 to 910 g of chocolate.
2. Place two-thirds of the chocolate in a double boiler or in a metal bowl set over a saucepan of simmering water. Make sure the bottom of the bowl is not touching the water. Place a candy thermometer in the chocolate.
3. Let the chocolate melt, stirring frequently with a rubber spatula to ensure even melting.
4. Do not let the temperature of the chocolate exceed 120°F/49°C for dark chocolate or 105°F/41°C for milk or white chocolate. When the chocolate has fully melted, remove the bowl from the heat.
5. Add the remaining one-third of the chocolate a little at a time. Stir each addition to let it fully melt and incorporate before adding more.
6. Check to see if the chocolate has cooled to about 82°F/28°C. If it is too warm, keep stirring and let it cool some more. If it is cooler, you can begin reheating the chocolate per the next step.
7. At 82°F/28°C, place the bowl back in the double boiler or over the saucepan and reheat the chocolate. For dark chocolate, reheat to a temperature of 88°F to 91°F/ 31°C to 33°C. For milk and white chocolate, reheat to a temperature of 85°F to 87°F/29°C to 31°C. Remove the bowl from the heat once the chocolate has reached the right temperature.

8. Take a small spoonful of chocolate and spread it out on a piece of parchment paper. If it dries quickly, with a glossy finish and no streaks, the chocolate is in temper. If it looks dull or blotchy, it has not been tempered properly. You will need to retemper. Place the bowl back over the saucepan of simmering water and melt per step 3. Follow the rest of the steps to retemper. (You will need to chop up extra unmelted chocolate to add to the mixture.)

Reasons why chocolate may not have tempered properly:

- You may have cooled or heated the chocolate to the wrong temperatures. If you do not cool the chocolate enough, the cocoa butter crystals may not form correctly. If you heat the chocolate higher than the indicated temperatures, you will bring the chocolate out of temper, and it will essentially be just regular melted chocolate. Be sure you have an accurate thermometer.

- Although the temperature ranges given should work for most chocolates, each brand and type of chocolate has different percentages of ingredients, and so will behave slightly differently when melted. You may have to experiment to find the right temperature for the chocolate you are using. However, it should not fall too far out of the given ranges. If you are using professional-quality chocolate, sometimes the temperatures for tempering are listed on the packaging. Higher-quality chocolates are generally easier to temper, because they use better ingredients and a higher percentage of cocoa butter. You should look for the best chocolate you can afford; it can make a big difference in your candies.

- Heat and humidity affect the chocolate tempering process adversely. In hot weather, it can be difficult to keep melted chocolate at the right temperature. Humidity is an even worse enemy to chocolate; the excess moisture interferes with the tempering process, and the chocolate may not set up properly. It's best to temper chocolate on a cool, dry day. If you have air-conditioning or a dehumidifier, it's worth a try. Chocolate, whether melted or in its finished form, performs and keeps best in a consistently cool environment.

Once melted chocolate is in temper, it needs to be used quickly before it cools and sets. If it cools to between 85°F and 87°F/29°C and 30°C, and is still slightly liquid, you can reheat it to a more liquid consistency. If it has completely cooled and solidified, you will need to melt and retemper it.

The easiest way to reheat tempered chocolate is to place it back over the double boiler or saucepan of simmering water for a few moments. The key point to remember is that chocolate cannot be heated above certain temperatures, or it will go out of temper. For dark chocolate, reheat to a temperature of 88°F to 91°F/31°C to 33°C. For milk and white chocolate, reheat to a temperature of 85°F to 87°F/29°C to 30°C. If you are able to keep your chocolate within these temperature ranges, the chocolate should stay in temper and be liquid enough to use.

When reheating tempered chocolate, be careful to leave the bowl of chocolate over the heat for only 5 to 10 seconds at a time. Stir the chocolate thoroughly and check the temperature before placing it back on the heat. Never leave a bowl of tempered chocolate over a saucepan of simmering water to "keep it warm"; it will quickly become too hot.

EQUIPMENT AND TOOLS

CANDY FUNNEL
A candy funnel is a funnel with a hole at the pointed end and a rod to help control the flow of hot sugar out the hole. This tool is quite helpful in allowing you precise control in filling lollipop molds without spilling hot sugar everywhere. You can find them online (see Resources, page 93) or sometimes at kitchen supply stores. As an alternative to a candy funnel, you can use a heatproof container with a spout for easy pouring. Silicone ones are best because it's easiest to clean hardened sugar off them.

CANDY THERMOMETER
A properly calibrated candy thermometer is crucial to sugar work, since a few degrees can mean the difference between caramel and charcoal. Make sure that it's a true candy thermometer that can go up to at least 400°F/200°C. The traditional flat, analog candy thermometers with a bulb and markings for different sugar stages work fine; for modernist types, a digital thermometer with a long metal probe also works and can be more precise than trying to read the temperature on an analog thermometer.

MEASURING TOOLS
Liquid ingredients in this book should be measured out in a liquid measuring cup. Dry ingredients can be measured out with measuring cups and spoons, but using a scale will give you the best results. Digital scales are inexpensive these days; make sure yours is accurate to the gram.

MIXING SPATULAS AND SPOONS
Your mixing tools need to withstand very high temperatures, so don't use plastic or metal spoons, which conduct heat and could burn your hand. Wooden spoons will work, as will specially designated high-heat silicone spatulas.

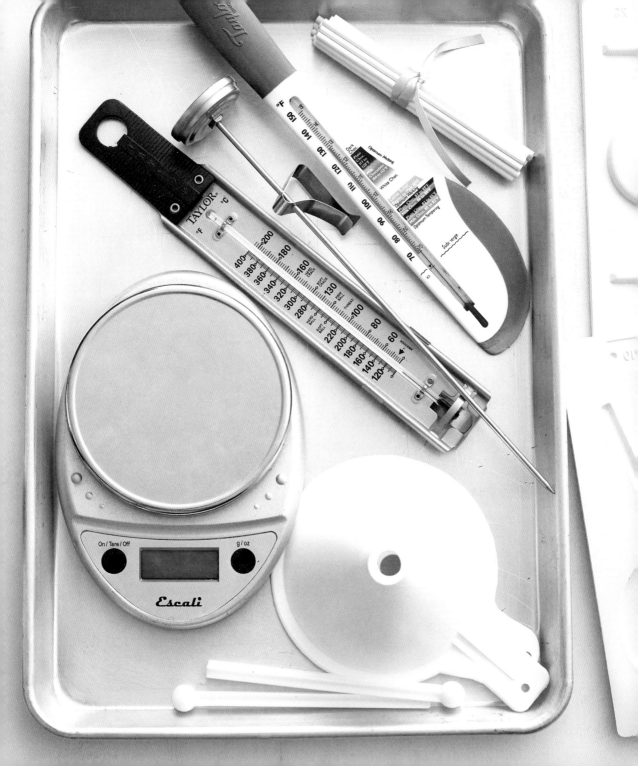

MOLDS

You can find candy molds in kitchenware and craft stores, but the widest variety is available online (see Resources, page 93, for a partial list). For sugar and caramel lollipops, be sure the molds you select are designated for making hard candy; other molds may not stand up to the extreme temperatures of molten sugar. For chocolate lollipops, you can use either hard-candy molds or chocolate molds. Most of the recipes in this book were tested in both 1½-in-/4-cm-diameter molds and 2-in-/5-cm-diameter molds.

OVEN MITTS

Candy making involves cooking sugar to extremely high temperatures, so take precautions to avoid accidents. It's wise to don a pair of oven mitts—thick cotton insulates best—to protect your hands when pouring out the lollipop mixture from the hot saucepan.

PARCHMENT PAPER

Lollipops won't stick to parchment paper. Sheets of parchment paper are useful for placing chocolate-dipped lollipops to set, or just to lay out unmolded lollipops before you package them up.

POTS AND PANS

The best vessel for cooking sugar is a heavy-bottom stainless-steel saucepan, preferably one that holds 3 to 4 qt/2.8 to 3.8 L. You want the pan to be sturdy so it doesn't warp under high heat, and you want enough capacity so it doesn't overflow with hot bubbling sugar. A copper pot is also an effective choice for cooking sugar, but copper can be expensive and is not necessary. Do not use an aluminum pan, as it can react with acidic ingredients.

SUGAR

LOLLIPOPS

This base recipe can be used with the flavorings and colorings of your choice to create your perfect lollipop. You don't even need molds if the lollipop-making urge strikes suddenly; see the variations for simple alternative ways to form lollipops.

THE BASIC LOLLIPOP

1   Coat the lollipop molds lightly with nonstick cooking spray. Place lollipop sticks in the molds.
2   Combine the sugar, water, and corn syrup in a large, heavy saucepan. Bring to a boil over medium-high heat.
3   Continue cooking until the mixture reaches 300°F/149°C (hard-crack stage). Immediately remove the saucepan from the heat.
4   Add the candy flavoring and food coloring (if using) and stir to combine.
5   Pour the mixture into a heatproof measuring container with a spout, or a candy funnel. Divide the mixture among the prepared molds.
6   Let the lollipops cool and harden, about 15 minutes, before removing them from the molds.

1 cup/200 g sugar

½ cup/120 ml water

¼ cup/60 ml light corn syrup

½ to 1 tsp candy flavoring

Few drops food coloring (optional)

FREE-FORM LOLLIPOPS

Line several baking sheets with parchment paper.

Use a metal measuring spoon to carefully drop rounds of the candy mixture onto the prepared baking sheets. Place lollipop sticks in the lollipops before the candy sets completely.

COOKIE-CUTTER LOLLIPOPS

Line several baking sheets with parchment paper. Place several metal cookie cutters coated with nonstick cooking spray on each baking sheet.

Pour the candy mixture into the cookie cutters, about ¼ in/6 mm thick. Let set for a few minutes before removing the cutters. Place lollipop sticks in the lollipops before the candy sets completely.

YIELD

Makes about 24 small (1½-in/4-cm) or 10 big (2-in/5-cm) round lollipops

STORAGE

Store wrapped in cellophane bags, twist-tied shut, in a cool, dry place for up to 1 month.

RAINBOW SWIRL LOLLIPOPS

By playing around with food coloring before the lollipops set, you can make some beautiful designs. You can also use multiple colors for an even more striking effect. Thicker gel colorings work best because they are easier to guide around with a toothpick.

1 cup/200 g sugar

½ cup/120 ml water

¼ cup/60 ml light corn syrup

½ to 1 tsp candy flavoring or 1 tsp vanilla extract

Food coloring in various colors

1 Coat the lollipop molds lightly with nonstick cooking spray. Place lollipop sticks in the molds.

2 Combine the sugar, water, and corn syrup in a large, heavy saucepan. Bring to a boil over medium-high heat.

3 Continue cooking until the mixture reaches 300°F/ 149°C (hard-crack stage). Immediately remove the saucepan from the heat.

4 Add the candy flavoring and stir to combine.

5 Pour the mixture into a heatproof measuring container with a spout, or a candy funnel. Divide the mixture among the prepared molds.

6 Working quickly, add a drop of food coloring to each lollipop. Use a toothpick or wooden skewer to swirl the food coloring around. You can add more drops or different colors as desired.

7 Let the lollipops cool and harden, about 15 minutes, before removing them from the molds.

YIELD

Makes about 24 small (1¼-in/4-cm) or 10 big (2-in/5-cm) round lollipops

STORAGE

Store wrapped in cellophane bags, twist-tied shut, in a cool, dry place for up to 1 month.

ROOT BEER LOLLIPOPS

The root beer candy flavoring I used imparted a true, pleasant root beer taste to these lollipops, but if you want to go really intense, you can use real root beer concentrate. I prefer McCormick's—it has strong sassafras and molasses notes and makes for wonderfully dark lollipops.

1 cup/200 g sugar

½ cup/120 ml water

¼ cup/60 ml light corn syrup

1 Tbsp vanilla bean paste

1 tsp root beer concentrate

1 Coat the lollipop molds lightly with nonstick cooking spray. Place lollipop sticks in the molds.
2 Combine the sugar, water, and corn syrup in a large, heavy saucepan. Bring to a boil over medium-high heat.
3 Continue cooking until the mixture reaches 300°F/149°C (hard-crack stage). Immediately remove the saucepan from the heat.
4 Stir in the vanilla bean paste and root beer concentrate.
5 Pour the mixture into a heatproof measuring container with a spout, or a candy funnel. Divide the mixture among the prepared molds.
6 Let the lollipops cool and harden, about 15 minutes, before removing them from the molds.

YIELD
Makes about 24 small (1½-in/4-cm) or 10 big (2-in/5-cm) round lollipops

STORAGE
Store wrapped in cellophane bags, twist-tied shut, in a cool, dry place for up to 1 month.

You can use your favorite tea in this recipe. The amount of sugar used in making lollipops can overwhelm more subtle flavors, so let the tea steep for longer than normal to intensify the flavor, 6 to 8 minutes for most teas. Also, if you're using tea meant for making iced tea, don't add any ice, as it will only dilute the flavor.

1   Coat the lollipop molds lightly with nonstick cooking spray. Place lollipop sticks in the molds.
2   Combine the sugar, tea, and corn syrup in a large, heavy saucepan. Bring to a boil over medium-high heat.
3   Continue cooking until the mixture reaches 300°F/ 149°C (hard-crack stage). Immediately remove the saucepan from the heat.
4   Pour the mixture into a heatproof measuring container with a spout, or a candy funnel. Divide the mixture among the prepared molds.
5   Let the lollipops cool and harden, about 15 minutes, before removing them from the molds.

PEACH ICED TEA LOLLIPOPS

1 cup/200 g sugar

1 cup/240 ml brewed peach tea

¼ cup/60 ml light corn syrup

YIELD

Makes about 24 small (1½-in/4-cm) or 10 big (2-in/5-cm) round lollipops

STORAGE

Store wrapped in cellophane bags, twist-tied shut, in a cool, dry place for up to 1 month.

This delicately pink lollipop is perfect for Valentine's Day. Rose syrup can be found at many Indian and Middle Eastern groceries and gives the lollipops a lovely pink hue without any other additional coloring needed. Be sure you use rose petals that haven't been sprayed with pesticides. If you can't find mini roses, you can cut up regular-size rose petals into pieces that will fit in the lollipops.

ROSEWATER-SAFFRON LOLLIPOPS

1 Coat the lollipop molds lightly with nonstick cooking spray. Place lollipop sticks in the molds.

2 Combine the sugar, water, corn syrup, and the ¼ tsp saffron in a large, heavy saucepan. Bring to a boil over medium-high heat.

3 Continue cooking until the mixture reaches 300°F/ 149°C (hard-crack stage). Immediately remove the saucepan from the heat.

4 Stir in the rosewater and rose syrup.

5 Pour the mixture into a heatproof measuring container with a spout, or a candy funnel. Divide the mixture among the prepared molds.

6 Using a stick, press a couple of rose petals and saffron threads into each lollipop.

7 Let the lollipops cool and harden, about 15 minutes, before removing them from the molds.

1 cup/200 g sugar

½ cup/120 ml water

¼ cup/60 ml light corn syrup

¼ tsp saffron threads, plus
saffron threads
for each lollipop

1 tsp rosewater

1 tsp rose syrup

Couple of mini rose petals for each lollipop

YIELD
Makes about 24 small (1½-in/4-cm) or 10 big (2-in/5-cm) round lollipops

STORAGE
Store wrapped in cellophane bags, twist-tied shut, in a cool, dry place for up to 1 month.

CINNAMON RED-HOT LOLLIPOPS

1 cup/200 g sugar

½ cup/120 ml water

¼ cup/60 ml light corn syrup

¾ tsp cinnamon oil

Few drops red food coloring

If you are a fan of little cinnamon candies, these lollipops are like a large version of those spicy sweets. If you want to make small individual pieces, try making this recipe in a jewel mold (see Resources, page 93).

1 Coat the lollipop molds lightly with nonstick cooking spray. Place lollipop sticks in the molds.

2 Combine the sugar, water, and corn syrup in a large, heavy saucepan. Bring to a boil over medium-high heat.

3 Continue cooking until the mixture reaches 300°F/149°C (hard-crack stage). Immediately remove the saucepan from the heat.

4 Add the cinnamon oil and food coloring and stir to combine. (Be careful to keep your face away from the pan, as the fumes can sting your eyes.)

5 Pour the mixture into a heatproof measuring container with a spout, or a candy funnel. Divide the mixture among the prepared molds.

6 Let the lollipops cool and harden, about 15 minutes, before removing them from the molds.

YIELD

Makes about 24 small (1½-in/4-cm) or 10 big (2-in/5-cm) round lollipops

STORAGE

Store wrapped in cellophane bags, twist-tied shut, in a cool, dry place for up to 1 month.

These lollipops are reminiscent of a popular confection with a piece of bubble gum hidden inside a candy shell. Experiment with different combinations of your favorite bubble gum and lollipop flavors.

BUBBLE GUM LOLLIPOPS

1 Coat the lollipop molds lightly with nonstick cooking spray. Cut the bubble gum into pieces small enough to fit into the molds (for a 1½-in/4-cm mold, use ½-in/12-mm pieces). Place a piece of bubble gum on the end of each lollipop stick and place the sticks in the molds. Be sure the bubble-gum pieces are also flat enough that they don't stick up beyond the mold so the candy mixture will cover them.

2 Combine the sugar, water, and corn syrup in a large, heavy saucepan. Bring to a boil over medium-high heat.

3 Continue cooking until the mixture reaches 300°F/149°C (hard-crack stage). Immediately remove the saucepan from the heat.

4 Add the bubble-gum oil and food coloring (if using) and stir to combine. (Be careful to keep your face away from the pan, as the fumes can sting your eyes.)

5 Pour the mixture into a heatproof measuring container with a spout, or a candy funnel. Divide the mixture among the prepared molds.

6 Let the lollipops cool and harden, about 15 minutes, before removing them from the molds.

1 pack soft bubble gum such as Bubble Yum

1 cup/200 g sugar

½ cup/120 ml water

¼ cup/60 ml light corn syrup

½ tsp bubble-gum oil

Few drops food coloring (optional)

YIELD

Makes about 24 small (1½-in/4-cm) or 10 big (2-in/5-cm) round lollipops

STORAGE

Store wrapped in cellophane bags, twist-tied shut, in a cool, dry place for up to 1 month.

CHRISTMAS PEPPERMINT LOLLIPOPS

One way to get creative with your lollipops is to make them in different shaped molds. For an ideal holiday sweet, make these lollipops in snowflake molds. Or, instead of using lollipop sticks, lay lengths of ribbon in each mold. You can then hang the lollipop snowflakes as decorations around the house.

1 cup/200 g sugar

½ cup/120 ml water

¼ cup/60 ml light corn syrup

½ tsp peppermint oil

Few drops blue food coloring (optional)

Disco dust for sprinkling

1 Coat the lollipop molds lightly with nonstick cooking spray. Place lollipop sticks in the molds.
2 Combine the sugar, water, and corn syrup in a large, heavy saucepan. Bring to a boil over medium-high heat.
3 Continue cooking until the mixture reaches 300°F/149°C (hard-crack stage). Immediately remove the saucepan from the heat.
4 Add the peppermint oil and food coloring (if using) and stir to combine. (Be careful to keep your face away from the pan, as the fumes can sting your eyes.)
5 Pour the mixture into a heatproof measuring container with a spout, or a candy funnel. Divide the mixture among the prepared molds.
6 Sprinkle a pinch of disco dust over each lollipop.
7 Let the lollipops cool and harden, about 15 minutes, before removing them from the molds.

YIELD

Makes about 24 small (1½-in/4-cm) or 10 big (2-in/5-cm) round lollipops

STORAGE

Store wrapped in cellophane bags, twist-tied shut, in a cool, dry place for up to 1 month.

As a kid, I was a big fan of those lemon candies covered in an ultrasour powder that made your mouth pucker up. Citric acid gives the same effect to these lollipops. You can use more citric acid in the sour powder if you like your candies really, really sour.

SUPER LEMON LOLLIPOPS

FOR THE LOLLIPOPS

1 Coat the lollipop molds lightly with nonstick cooking spray. Place lollipop sticks in the molds.
2 Combine the sugar, water, and corn syrup in a large, heavy saucepan. Bring to a boil over medium-high heat.
3 Continue cooking until the mixture reaches 300°F/ 149°C (hard-crack stage). Immediately remove the saucepan from the heat.
4 Add the citric acid, lemon oil, and food coloring and stir to combine. (Be careful to keep your face away from the pan, as the fumes can sting your eyes.)
5 Pour the mixture into a heatproof measuring container with a spout, or a candy funnel. Divide the mixture among the prepared molds.
6 Let the lollipops cool and harden, about 15 minutes, before removing them from the molds.

FOR THE SOUR POWDER

7 Mix the confectioners' sugar and citric acid together in a bowl.
8 Dip the lollipops in the mixture to coat.

LOLLIPOPS

1 cup/200 g sugar

½ cup/120 ml water

¼ cup/60 ml light corn syrup

1¼ tsp citric acid

¾ tsp lemon oil

Few drops yellow food coloring

SOUR POWDER

½ cup/50 g confectioners' sugar

2 tsp citric acid

YIELD
Makes about 24 small (1½-in/4-cm) or 10 big (2-in/5-cm) round lollipops

STORAGE
Store wrapped in cellophane bags, twist-tied shut, in a cool, dry place for up to 1 month.

CHAMPAGNE AND GLITTER LOLLIPOPS

These lollipops are ideal for New Year's Eve, weddings, or any festive celebration. You don't need to break out your priciest champagne for this recipe but do use one you enjoy.

1 cup/200 g sugar

½ cup/120 ml champagne

¼ cup/60 ml light corn syrup

Few drops food coloring (optional)

⅛ tsp edible glitter dust, plus more for sprinkling

1   Coat the lollipop molds lightly with nonstick cooking spray. Place lollipop sticks in the molds.

2   Combine the sugar, champagne, and corn syrup in a large, heavy saucepan. Bring to a boil over medium-high heat.

3   Continue cooking until the mixture reaches 300°F/ 149°C (hard-crack stage). Immediately remove the saucepan from the heat.

4   Add the food coloring (if using) and the ⅛ tsp glitter dust and stir to combine.

5   Pour the mixture into a heatproof measuring container with a spout, or a candy funnel. Divide the mixture among the prepared molds.

6   Sprinkle a pinch more glitter dust over the top of each lollipop.

7   Let the lollipops cool and harden, about 15 minutes, before removing them from the molds.

YIELD

Makes about 24 small (1½-in/4-cm) or 10 big (2-in/5-cm) round lollipops

STORAGE

Store wrapped in cellophane bags, twist-tied shut, in a cool, dry place for up to 1 month.

BEER LOLLIPOPS

⅔ cup/165 ml full-flavored beer

3 or 4 hop cones

1 cup/200 g sugar

¼ cup/60 ml light corn syrup

Few drops food coloring (optional)

YIELD

Makes about 24 small (1½-in/4-cm) or 10 big (2-in/5-cm) round lollipops

STORAGE

Store wrapped in cellophane bags, twist-tied shut, in a cool, dry place for up to 1 month.

This is a great recipe for experimentation: Try using your favorite beers to make these lollipops; the stronger and more full-flavored the beer, the better the results. Because the sugar can dilute the beer flavor, hops are added to help intensify the flavor. You can adjust the number of hop cones and their steeping time depending on how strong a flavor you want. Use a saucepan with a capacity of at least 5 qt/4.7 L, as the boiling beer can become very foamy and you don't want it to overflow.

1 Coat the lollipop molds lightly with nonstick cooking spray. Place lollipop sticks in the molds.
2 Combine the beer and hops in a heavy saucepan with a capacity of at least 5 qt/4.7 L. Bring to a boil, remove from the heat, and let steep for 10 minutes. Strain the beer and discard the hops.
3 Return the strained beer to the saucepan, stir in the sugar and corn syrup, and bring to a boil over medium-high heat.
4 Continue cooking until the mixture reaches 300°F/149°C (hard-crack stage). Immediately remove the saucepan from the heat.
5 Add the food coloring (if using) and stir to combine.
6 Pour the mixture into a heatproof measuring container with a spout, or a candy funnel. Divide the mixture among the prepared molds.
7 Let the lollipops cool and harden, about 15 minutes, before removing them from the molds.

These throat soothers are wonderful to have on hand when you or someone else has a sore throat. Try using your favorite honey to make these.

HONEY-CHAMOMILE LOLLIPOPS

1 Coat the lollipop molds lightly with nonstick cooking spray. Place lollipop sticks in the molds.

2 Combine the sugar, tea, corn syrup, and honey in a large, heavy saucepan. Bring to a boil over medium-high heat.

3 Continue cooking until the mixture reaches 300°F/149°C (hard-crack stage). Immediately remove the saucepan from the heat.

4 Pour the mixture into a heatproof measuring container with a spout, or a candy funnel. Divide the mixture among the prepared molds.

5 Let the lollipops cool and harden, about 15 minutes, before removing them from the molds.

1 cup/200 g sugar

1 cup/240 ml brewed chamomile tea

¼ cup/60 ml light corn syrup

¼ cup/85 g honey

YIELD
Makes about 24 small (1½-in/4-cm) or 10 big (2-in/5-cm) round lollipops

STORAGE
Store wrapped in cellophane bags, twist-tied shut, in a cool, dry place for up to 1 month.

MAPLE, BACON, AND WALNUT LOLLIPOPS

1 cup/200 g sugar

½ cup/120 ml water

¼ cup/60 ml light corn syrup

¼ cup/60 ml maple syrup

About 2 Tbsp bacon bits or finely chopped cooked bacon

About 2 Tbsp finely chopped toasted walnuts

YIELD
Makes about 24 small (1½-in/4-cm) or 10 big (2-in/5-cm) round lollipops

STORAGE
Store wrapped in cellophane bags, twist-tied shut, in a cool, dry place for up to 1 month.

Maple syrup comes in several varieties, from light to dark. The darker the syrup, the more intense the maple flavor, which is what you want for these lollipops The bacon and walnut pieces turn a simple lollipop into a sweet and savory candy for the adventurous.

1 Coat the lollipop molds lightly with nonstick cooking spray. Place lollipop sticks in the molds.
2 Combine the sugar, water, corn syrup, and maple syrup in a large, heavy saucepan. Bring to a boil over medium-high heat.
3 Continue cooking until the mixture reaches 300°F/ 149°C (hard-crack stage). Immediately remove the saucepan from the heat.
4 Pour the mixture into a heatproof measuring container with a spout, or a candy funnel. Divide the mixture among the prepared molds.
5 Sprinkle a few bits of bacon and walnuts over the top of each lollipop.
6 Let the lollipops cool and harden, about 15 minutes, before removing them from the molds.

PURE MAPLE LOLLIPOPS
When you have a really great maple syrup you want to show off, you don't need any other ingredients. Simply cook ½ cup/120 ml maple syrup to 290°F/143°C, and pour into the prepared lollipop molds.

These lollipops pack an intense vanilla wallop from the combination of vanilla bean paste and ground vanilla beans. Ground vanilla beans are available in some specialty grocery stores, but if you can't find them, you can simply cut open a vanilla bean and scrape out the seeds inside. All the vanilla gives these lollipops a sweet, almost cotton candy flavor; the addition of sea salt provides a counterpoint that makes these lollipops positively addictive.

DOUBLE VANILLA LOLLIPOPS

1 cup/200 g sugar

½ cup/120 ml water

¼ cup/60 ml light corn syrup

1 Tbsp vanilla bean paste

¼ tsp ground vanilla bean

Sea salt for sprinkling

1 Coat the lollipop molds lightly with nonstick cooking spray. Place lollipop sticks in the molds.

2 Combine the sugar, water, and corn syrup in a large, heavy saucepan. Bring to a boil over medium-high heat.

3 Continue cooking until the mixture reaches 300°F/ 149°C (hard-crack stage). Immediately remove the saucepan from the heat.

4 Add the vanilla bean paste and ground vanilla bean and stir to combine.

5 Pour the mixture into a heatproof measuring container with a spout, or a candy funnel. Divide the mixture among the prepared molds.

6 Sprinkle a few grains of sea salt over the top of each lollipop.

7 Let the lollipops cool and harden, about 15 minutes, before removing them from the molds.

YIELD

Makes about 24 small (1½-in/4-cm) or 10 big (2-in/5-cm) round lollipops

STORAGE

Store wrapped in cellophane bags, twist-tied shut, in a cool, dry place for up to 1 month.

Mango and chili is a sweet-spicy combination popular in many Asian and Latin American countries. In Mexico, they take it a step further with Tajín, a combination of chili powder, salt, and lime juice. You can add the Tajín seasoning to the lollipop mix or dip the hardened lollipops into the powder for an extra kick. Tajín powder is available at Mexican grocery stores; if you can't find it, you can substitute regular chili powder.

1 Coat the lollipop molds lightly with nonstick cooking spray. Place lollipop sticks in the molds.
2 Combine the sugar, mango nectar, and corn syrup in a large, heavy saucepan. Bring to a boil over medium-high heat.
3 Continue cooking until the mixture reaches 275°F/135°C (soft-crack stage). Immediately remove the saucepan from the heat.
4 Add the candy flavoring and stir to combine.
5 Pour the mixture into a heatproof measuring container with a spout, or a candy funnel. Fill each of the molds halfway.
6 Sprinkle the Tajín seasoning over the lollipops. Pour the rest of the mixture over the lollipops, filling the molds completely.
7 Let the lollipops cool and harden, about 15 minutes, before removing them from the molds.

MANGO-CHILI LOLLIPOPS

1 cup/200 g sugar

1 cup/240 ml mango nectar

¼ cup/60 ml light corn syrup

½ tsp mango candy flavoring

1 Tbsp Tajín Clásico seasoning

YIELD
Makes about 24 small (1½-in/4-cm) or 10 big (2-in/5-cm) round lollipops

STORAGE
Store wrapped in cellophane bags, twist-tied shut, in a cool, dry place for up to 1 month.

EDIBLE PAPER LOLLIPOPS

Edible paper is a great way to truly personalize your lollipops. Edible paper can be easily found on the Internet (see Resources, page 93) and comes preprinted with images or in blank sheets that you can decorate. This is an ideal way to make lollipop favors for weddings, showers, or just to fancy up a party.

Edible paper

1 cup/200 g sugar

½ cup/120 ml water

¼ cup/60 ml light corn syrup

½ to 1 tsp candy flavoring

Few drops food coloring (optional)

1 Prepare the edible paper with the images you want and make sure it has been cut to fit the size lollipops you are making.

2 Coat the lollipop molds lightly with nonstick cooking spray. Place the edible paper pieces in each mold. Place lollipop sticks in the molds.

3 Combine the sugar, water, and corn syrup in a large, heavy saucepan. Bring to a boil over medium-high heat.

4 Continue cooking until the mixture reaches 300°F/149°C (hard-crack stage). Immediately remove the saucepan from the heat.

5 Add the candy flavoring and food coloring (if using) and stir to combine.

6 Pour the mixture into a heatproof measuring container with a spout, or a candy funnel. Divide the mixture among the prepared molds.

7 Let the lollipops cool and harden, about 15 minutes, before removing them from the molds.

YIELD
Makes about 24 small (1½-in/4-cm) or 10 big (2-in/5-cm) round lollipops

STORAGE
Store wrapped in cellophane bags, twist-tied shut, in a cool, dry place for up to 1 month.

SWEET AGAVE LOLLIPOPS

1 cup/200 g sugar

½ cup/120 ml water

¼ cup/60 ml agave syrup

Agave syrup is a popular substitute for corn syrup in baking. It makes beautiful pale golden lollipops that taste of sweet, mellow caramel. Agave is more sensitive to humidity than corn syrup is, so make sure to wrap the lollipops well and store them in a cool, dry place away from heat.

1 Coat the lollipop molds lightly with nonstick cooking spray. Place lollipop sticks in the molds.

2 Combine the sugar, water, and agave syrup in a large, heavy saucepan. Bring to a boil over medium-high heat.

3 Continue cooking until the mixture reaches 300°F/ 149°C (hard crack stage). Immediately remove the saucepan from the heat.

4 Pour the mixture into a heatproof measuring container with a spout, or a candy funnel. Divide the mixture among the prepared molds.

5 Let the lollipops cool and harden, about 15 minutes, before removing them from the molds.

AGAVE-ORANGE LOLLIPOPS
Add a couple drops of orange oil (not extract) to the lollipop syrup after you remove it from the heat. The floral citrus adds a bright complement to the caramel notes of the agave.

YIELD

Makes about 24 small (1½-in/4-cm) or 10 big (2-in/5-cm) round lollipops

STORAGE

Store wrapped in cellophane bags, twist-tied shut, in a cool, dry place for up to 1 month.

Golden syrup, also known as light treacle, is a British staple; it is used both in baking and as a syrup, drizzled over tarts and puddings. It's often listed as a substitute for corn syrup, but golden syrup has much more character. These lollipops have a wonderfully buttery, toasty flavor and a tantalizing dark amber hue.

GOLDEN SYRUP LOLLIPOPS

1 cup/200 g sugar

½ cup/120 ml water

¼ cup/60 ml golden syrup

1 Coat the lollipop molds lightly with nonstick cooking spray. Place lollipop sticks in the molds.

2 Combine the sugar, water, and golden syrup in a large, heavy saucepan. Bring to a boil over medium-high heat.

3 Continue cooking until the mixture reaches 300°F/ 149°C (hard-crack stage). Immediately remove the saucepan from the heat.

4 Pour the mixture into a heatproof measuring container with a spout, or a candy funnel. Divide the mixture among the prepared molds.

5 Let the lollipops cool and harden, about 15 minutes, before removing them from the molds.

YIELD

Makes about 24 small (1½-in/4-cm) or 10 big (2-in/5-cm) round lollipops

STORAGE

Store wrapped in cellophane bags, twist-tied shut, in a cool, dry place for up to 1 month.

Barley sugar candy is a traditional British sweet made simply with barley water and sugar. The barley gives the candy a very clear, glasslike appearance. In Victorian England, the candy was often made in fanciful molds to appeal to children, so it's often known as barley toy candy or clear toy candy. Try not to disturb the barley as it's cooking to keep it as clear as possible, but even if it's not perfectly clear the results will still be delicious.

BARLEY SUGAR LOLLIPOPS

½ cup/100 g pearl barley

6 cups/1.4 L water

4 cups/800 g sugar

Pinch of cream of tartar

1   Combine the pearl barley and water in a large, tall stockpot. Bring just to a boil over medium-high heat.

2   Turn the heat to low and keep the mixture just below a simmer for about 2 hours. Do not stir the mixture; you want to keep the water as clear of barley sediment as possible.

3   Strain the barley water into a large container. Measure out 1 cup/240 ml of barley water to use (some of the water will have evaporated).

4   Coat the lollipop molds lightly with nonstick cooking spray. Place lollipop sticks in the molds.

5   Combine the 1 cup/240 ml barley water, the sugar, and cream of tartar in a heavy saucepan with a capacity of at least 6 qt/5.7 L. Bring to a boil over medium-high heat.

6   Continue cooking until the mixture reaches 300°F/149°C (hard-crack stage). Immediately remove the saucepan from the heat.

7   Pour the mixture into a heatproof measuring container with a spout, or a candy funnel. Divide the mixture among the prepared molds.

8   Let the lollipops cool and harden, about 15 minutes, before removing them from the molds.

YIELD

Makes about 24 small (1½-in/4-cm) or 10 big (2-in/5-cm) round lollipops

STORAGE

Store wrapped in cellophane bags, twist-tied shut, in a cool, dry place for up to 1 month.

ROCK CANDY

Sugar for coating
the skewers, plus
6 cups/1.2 kg

2 cups/480 ml water

Few drops food
coloring (optional)

Few drops candy
flavoring (optional)

Rock candy is perhaps the simplest form of candy: it's purely large crystals of sugar clustered together on a stick, and nothing else. Called rock candy because the crystals resemble rock formations, this candy is popularly made as a science experiment to help show how crystals form. If you are doing this with kids, they will especially love adding different colors and flavors to the mixture to get some wild rock candy. You will need 12 wooden skewers to make these.

1 Find several 1-qt/960-ml glass jars that have as large an opening at the top as possible and are tall enough to accommodate the wooden skewers you are using for the candy. (Wide-mouth canning jars work well.) Be sure they are completely clean and dry.

2 Wet the wooden skewers in water, roll them in sugar to coat, and let dry. (These are the seed crystals that will encourage more sugar crystals to form on the skewer.)

3 Bring the 2 cups/480 ml water to a boil in a large saucepan over high heat.

4 Add the 6 cups sugar, 1 cup/200 g at a time, stirring to ensure it is fully dissolved. The sugar should be completely dissolved, and the mixture clear. Boil the mixture for about 10 minutes.

5 Add the food coloring (if using) and candy flavoring (if using) and stir to combine.

6 Let the solution cool for about 10 minutes. Pour the sugar solution into the jars, filling them about two-thirds full.

7 There are a couple ways to suspend the skewers in the jars. One is to use a piece of Styrofoam large enough to cover the jar. Stick the skewers about 1 in/ 2.5 cm apart in the Styrofoam, then flip the Styrofoam over and place over the jar so the skewers are now immersed in the solution. Another method is to use a clothespin or clip that is long enough to rest across the opening of the jar without falling in. Secure the skewers in the clip and lay the clip across the jar opening. For both methods, make sure the skewers are suspended about 1 in/2.5 cm from the bottom of the jar and that the skewers are spaced about 1 in/2.5 cm apart to allow the crystals room to grow. You can probably fit about four skewers per jar.

8 Cover the jar with foil or plastic wrap. Place the jar somewhere at room temperature where it can be undisturbed for the next 5 to 7 days.

CONTINUED

YIELD

Makes about 12 rock candy pops

STORAGE

Store wrapped in cellophane bags, twist-tied shut, in a cool, dry place for up to 1 month.

9 Over the next few days, crystals will start forming and growing up the skewers. Leave the sticks undisturbed to allow the biggest crystals to form. (If no crystals form within a couple of days, the solution may not have been saturated enough. You can try again by starting over and remaking the solution with an extra ½ cup/100 g sugar.)

10 Remove the candy when you are satisfied with the amount of crystals grown on the skewers.

CARAMEL

LOLLIPOPS

When you make caramel, the amount of fat you add affects whether you'll get a luxurious creamy sauce or a chewy candy. Just a touch of butter and cream will give you these toothsome hard lollipops.

HARD CARAMEL LOLLIPOPS

1 Coat the lollipop molds lightly with nonstick cooking spray. Place lollipop sticks in the molds.
2 Combine the sugar, corn syrup, water, and salt in a large, heavy saucepan. Bring to a boil over medium-high heat.
3 While the sugar is cooking, heat the cream and vanilla in a separate small saucepan just to a boil. Turn the heat to low to keep the cream just warm.
4 Continue cooking the sugar mixture until it reaches 300°F/149°C (hard-crack stage). Immediately remove the saucepan from the heat.
5 Add the warmed cream slowly to the cooked sugar; be careful, as the mixture will boil up vigorously and settle back down.
6 Add the butter, a piece or two at a time, stirring to fully melt and incorporate. Divide the mixture among the prepared molds.
7 Let the lollipops cool and harden, about 15 minutes, before removing them from the molds.

BROWNED BUTTER–CARAMEL LOLLIPOPS

Place the butter in a small (8-in/20-cm) skillet and melt over medium heat, swirling occasionally, until it starts to turn brown and smells nutty. Do not let the butter get too dark or it will burn. Using a fine-mesh strainer, strain the butter into a clean bowl. Add the butter to the lollipop mixture with the cream.

1 cup/200 g sugar

¼ cup/60 ml light corn syrup

2 Tbsp water

½ tsp salt

¼ cup/60 ml heavy cream

½ tsp vanilla extract

1 Tbsp unsalted butter, cut into 4 pieces

YIELD
Makes about 24 small (1½-in/4-cm) or 10 big (2-in/5-cm) round lollipops

STORAGE
Store wrapped in cellophane bags, twist-tied shut, in a cool, dry place for up to 1 month.

FLEUR DE SEL, LAVENDER, AND CARAMEL LOLLIPOPS

Fleur de sel and lavender turn these caramels into a delicate, French-inspired confection. Fresh lavender will give you the best results; try to find some at a local farmers' market or nursery. You can also try infusing other herbs into the cream for the caramel.

1 cup/200 g sugar

¼ cup/60 ml light corn syrup

2 Tbsp water

Fleur de sel

¼ cup/60 ml heavy cream

1 Tbsp dried lavender buds

½ tsp vanilla extract

1 Tbsp unsalted butter, cut into 4 pieces

YIELD
Makes about 24 small (1½-in/4-cm) or 10 big (2-in/5-cm) round lollipops

STORAGE
Store wrapped in cellophane bags, twist-tied shut, in a cool, dry place for up to 1 month.

1 Coat the lollipop molds lightly with nonstick cooking spray. Place lollipop sticks in the molds.
2 Combine the sugar, corn syrup, water, and ½ tsp fleur de sel in a large, heavy saucepan. Bring to a boil over medium-high heat.
3 While the sugar is cooking, heat the cream, lavender buds, and vanilla in a separate small saucepan just to a boil. Turn the heat to low to keep the cream just warm.
4 Continue cooking the sugar mixture until it reaches 300°F/149°C (hard-crack stage). Immediately remove the saucepan from the heat.
5 Strain the warmed cream and add slowly to the cooked sugar; be careful, as the mixture will boil up vigorously and settle back down.
6 Add the butter, a piece or two at a time, stirring to fully melt and incorporate. Divide the mixture among the prepared molds.
7 Sprinkle some fleur de sel over the lollipops.
8 Let the lollipops cool and harden, about 15 minutes, before removing them from the molds.

ESPRESSO-CARAMEL LOLLIPOPS

These smoky, intense caramels make an ideal after-dinner sweet, or a late-morning pick-me-up, if you're so inclined.

1 cup/200 g sugar

¼ cup/60 ml light corn syrup

2 Tbsp water

½ tsp salt

¼ cup/60 ml heavy cream

1 tsp espresso powder

½ tsp vanilla extract

1 Tbsp unsalted butter, cut into 4 pieces

2 tsp dark rum

1. Coat the lollipop molds lightly with nonstick cooking spray. Place lollipop sticks in the molds.
2. Combine the sugar, corn syrup, water, and salt in a large, heavy saucepan. Bring to a boil over medium-high heat.
3. While the sugar is cooking, heat the cream, espresso powder, and vanilla in a separate small saucepan just to a boil. Turn the heat to low to keep the cream just warm.
4. Continue cooking the sugar mixture until it reaches 300°F/149°C (hard-crack stage). Immediately remove the saucepan from the heat.
5. Add the warmed cream slowly to the cooked sugar; be careful, as the mixture will boil up vigorously and settle back down.
6. Add the butter, a piece or two at a time, stirring to fully melt and incorporate. Add the rum. Divide the mixture among the prepared molds.
7. Let the lollipops cool and harden, about 15 minutes, before removing them from the molds.

YIELD
Makes about 24 small (1½-in/4-cm) or 10 big (2-in/5-cm) round lollipops

STORAGE
Store wrapped in cellophane bags, twist-tied shut, in a cool, dry place for up to 1 month.

Passion fruit and caramel are opposites that go together surprisingly well: tart versus sweet, fruity versus creamy.

PASSION FRUIT– CARAMEL LOLLIPOPS

1 Coat the lollipop molds lightly with nonstick cooking spray. Place lollipop sticks in the molds.

2 Combine the sugar, corn syrup, water, and salt in a large, heavy saucepan. Bring to a boil over medium-high heat.

3 While the sugar is cooking, heat the cream in a separate small saucepan just to a boil. Turn the heat to low to keep the cream just warm.

4 Continue cooking the sugar mixture until it reaches 300°F/149°C (hard-crack stage). Immediately remove the saucepan from the heat.

5 Add the warmed cream slowly to the cooked sugar; be careful, as the mixture will boil up vigorously and settle back down.

6 Add the butter, a piece or two at a time, stirring to fully melt and incorporate. Add the passion fruit purée and stir to incorporate. Reheat to about 250°F/121°C. Divide the mixture among the prepared molds.

7 Let the lollipops cool and harden, about 15 minutes, before removing them from the molds.

1 cup/200 g sugar

¼ cup/60 ml light corn syrup

2 Tbsp water

½ tsp salt

¼ cup/60 ml heavy cream

1 Tbsp unsalted butter, cut into 4 pieces

¼ cup/60 g passion fruit purée

YIELD
Makes about 24 small (1½-in/4-cm) or 10 big (2-in/5-cm) round lollipops

STORAGE
Store wrapped in cellophane bags, twist-tied shut, in a cool, dry place for up to 1 month.

PUMPKIN PIE SPICE–CARAMEL LOLLIPOPS

These lollipops are delicious on their own, or you can swirl one into your coffee to make your own pumpkin spice latte. A 2-in/5-cm lollipop will work nicely for a 12-oz/360-ml beverage. If you don't have pumpkin pie spice, you can substitute ¼ tsp each of ground allspice, cinnamon, ginger, and nutmeg.

½ cup/100 g granulated sugar

½ cup/100 g packed light brown sugar

¼ cup/60 ml light corn syrup

2 Tbsp water

½ tsp salt

¼ cup/60 ml heavy cream

1 tsp pumpkin pie spice

½ tsp vanilla extract

1 Tbsp unsalted butter, cut into 4 pieces

YIELD
Makes about 24 small (1½-in/4-cm) or 10 big (2-in/5-cm) round lollipops

STORAGE
Store wrapped in cellophane bags, twist-tied shut, in a cool, dry place for up to 1 month.

1 Coat the lollipop molds lightly with nonstick cooking spray. Place lollipop sticks in the molds.

2 Combine the granulated sugar, brown sugar, corn syrup, water, and salt in a large, heavy saucepan. Bring to a boil over medium-high heat.

3 While the sugar is cooking, heat the cream, pumpkin pie spice, and vanilla in a separate small saucepan just to a boil. Turn the heat to low to keep the cream just warm.

4 Continue cooking the sugar mixture until it reaches 300°F/149°C (hard-crack stage). Immediately remove the saucepan from the heat.

5 Add the warmed cream slowly to the cooked sugar; be careful, as the mixture will boil up vigorously and settle back down.

6 Add the butter, a piece or two at a time, stirring to fully melt and incorporate. Divide the mixture among the prepared molds.

7 Let the lollipops cool and harden, about 15 minutes, before removing them from the molds.

These are similar to old-fashioned butterscotch drops. Originally the vinegar was added to help prevent the sugar from crystallizing and to impart a bit of a tang to the finished butterscotch. Use distilled white vinegar to prevent the candy from turning dark or having too vinegary a taste.

GRANDMA'S BUTTER-SCOTCH LOLLIPOPS

1   Coat the lollipop molds lightly with nonstick cooking spray. Place lollipop sticks in the molds.
2   Combine the granulated sugar, brown sugar, water, corn syrup, vinegar, and salt in a large, heavy saucepan. Bring to a boil over medium-high heat.
3   Continue cooking the sugar mixture until it reaches 300°F/149°C (hard-crack stage). Immediately remove the saucepan from the heat.
4   Add the vanilla and stir to combine.
5   Pour the mixture into a heatproof measuring container with a spout, or a candy funnel. Divide the mixture among the prepared molds.
6   Let the lollipops cool and harden, about 15 minutes, before removing them from the molds.

½ cup/100 g granulated sugar

½ cup/100 g packed light brown sugar

½ cup/120 ml water

¼ cup/60 ml light corn syrup

1 Tbsp distilled white vinegar

½ tsp salt

1 tsp vanilla extract

YIELD
Makes about 24 small (1½-in/4-cm) or 10 big (2-in/5-cm) round lollipops

STORAGE
Store wrapped in cellophane bags, twist-tied shut, in a cool, dry place for up to 1 month.

DULCE DE LECHE SWIRL LOLLIPOPS

1 cup/200 g sugar

½ cup/120 ml water

¼ cup/60 ml light corn syrup

¼ cup/60 g dulce de leche, homemade (recipe follows) or store-bought

Edible glitter or disco dust for sprinkling

YIELD
Makes about 24 small (1½-in/4-cm) or 10 big (2-in/5-cm) round lollipops

STORAGE
Store wrapped in cellophane bags, twist-tied shut, in a cool, dry place for up to 1 month.

You can replace the dulce de leche with Nutella, chocolate, or basically anything that can be piped. Since these lollipops take a bit of coordination, pour out the lollipop mixture a little at a time and keep the remainder in the saucepan for easy preheating.

1 Coat the lollipop molds lightly with nonstick cooking spray. Place lollipop sticks in the molds.

2 Combine the sugar, water, and corn syrup in a large, heavy saucepan. Bring to a boil over medium-high heat.

3 Continue cooking the sugar mixture until it reaches 300°F/149°C (hard-crack stage). Immediately remove the saucepan from the heat.

4 Pour about half of the mixture into a heatproof measuring container with a spout, or a candy funnel. (Keep the remainder of the mixture in the hot saucepan. If it starts to set, place it over medium-high heat to rewarm.) Fill the prepared molds halfway with the mixture. Let sit for a couple minutes.

5 Spoon the dulce de leche into a zipper-lock bag and snip off one corner to make a small hole about ⅛ in/ 4 mm wide. Pipe a swirl of dulce de leche in the center of each lollipop, being careful not to get too close to the edges. Fill the molds with the rest of the mixture, covering the dulce de leche. Sprinkle with edible glitter.

6 Let the lollipops cool and harden, about 15 minutes, before removing them from the molds.

HOMEMADE DULCE DE LECHE
Pour a 14-oz/397-g can of condensed milk into a large metal bowl set over a saucepan of simmering water. Cook over low heat until it thickens and turns dark golden, stirring occasionally to prevent the bottom from burning. It may take a few hours for the dulce de leche to completely caramelize, but resist turning up the heat too high or the milk could burn. Let the dulce de leche cool and thicken before using.

Buttercrunch, or English toffee, usually comes in slabs, but it can easily be turned into a lollipop. It's best to make the buttercrunch lollipops in shallow molds (¼ in/6 mm deep or less), as they may be difficult to bite through if they're too thick. You can use molds bigger than 1½ in/4 cm in diameter, but again, make sure the thickness is ¼ in/6 mm or less.

1 Coat the lollipop molds lightly with nonstick cooking spray. Place lollipop sticks in the molds.
2 Combine the granulated sugar, brown sugar, butter, water, and salt in a medium saucepan. Cook over medium heat, stirring to combine, until the mixture comes to a boil.
3 Continue cooking without stirring until the mixture reaches 300°F/149°C (hard-crack stage). Immediately remove the saucepan from the heat.
4 Add the vanilla and baking soda and stir to combine.
5 Pour the mixture into the prepared molds. Let set completely, about 15 minutes.
6 When you are ready to dip the lollipops, temper the chocolate (see page 18). Line a baking sheet with parchment paper. Dip each lollipop in the chocolate and place on the prepared baking sheet; sprinkle with the almonds.
7 Let the lollipops set, about 20 minutes, before removing them from the parchment.

ALMOND BUTTER-CRUNCH LOLLIPOPS

¾ cup/150 g granulated sugar

½ cup/100 g packed light brown sugar

½ cup/115 g unsalted butter, cut into 1-in/2.5-cm pieces

2 Tbsp water

⅛ tsp salt

1 tsp vanilla extract

¼ tsp baking soda

12 oz/340 g bittersweet or semisweet chocolate

About ¾ cup/75 g slivered almonds, toasted and finely chopped

YIELD
Makes about 24 small (1½-in/4-cm) round lollipops

STORAGE
Store wrapped in cellophane bags, twist-tied shut, in a cool, dry place for up to 1 month.

Honeycomb toffee, also known as sponge candy, seafoam candy, or fairy food, is a fun science lesson: Baking soda added to hot sugar syrup causes bubbles of carbon dioxide to form. When the candy cools and solidifies, the trapped bubbles give it a crisp, spongelike texture.

It's best to use shallow lollipop molds (¼ in/6 mm deep or less), because this toffee can be quite hard and difficult to bite through if it's too thick. Although the transformation from hot syrup into sea foam–like mass is mesmerizing, it's still extremely hot sugar, so take the same care not to accidentally touch it.

HONEYCOMB TOFFEE LOLLIPOPS

2 cups/400 g sugar

½ cup/120 ml water

¼ cup/60 ml light corn syrup

¼ cup/60 ml honey

½ tsp salt

1 Tbsp baking soda, sifted

8 oz/225 g bittersweet chocolate

1   Coat the lollipop molds lightly with nonstick cooking spray. Place lollipop sticks in the molds. Line four baking sheets (rimmed is best) with parchment paper and place the molds on the baking sheets. (This will help catch any overflowing candy.)

2   Combine the sugar, water, corn syrup, honey, and salt in a large, heavy saucepan. Bring to a boil over medium-high heat.

3   Continue cooking the sugar mixture until it reaches 300°F/149°C (hard-crack stage). Immediately remove the saucepan from the heat.

4   Add the baking soda and stir carefully to combine. The mixture will bubble up violently, so be *very* careful.

5   Pour the mixture into the molds, again being careful not to touch it. (Some of the candy may bubble out, so you might get some irregularly shaped lollipops.) Let set completely, about 10 minutes.

6   When you are ready to dip the lollipops, temper the chocolate (see page 18). Line a baking sheet with parchment paper. Dip each lollipop in the chocolate and place on the prepared baking sheet.

7   Let the lollipops set, about 15 minutes, before removing them from the parchment.

YIELD

Makes about 48 small (1½-in/4-cm) lollipops

STORAGE

Store wrapped in cellophane bags, twist-tied shut, in a cool, dry place for up to 1 month.

CHOCOLATE

LOLLIPOPS

This French confection is traditionally eaten at Christmas. The classic toppings of almonds, hazelnuts, dried figs, and raisins correspond to the colors of the robes worn by four Catholic mendicant orders. If you don't have the time to temper chocolate, you can simply make these with melted chocolate but be sure to keep them refrigerated and consume within 2 days. Try using twigs (washed and dried) instead of lollipop sticks for an unusual, rustic look.

MENDIANTS ON A STICK

8 oz/225 g bittersweet chocolate

About 4 oz/115 g chopped dried fruits and nuts, such as raisins, dried figs, dried cranberries, almonds, hazelnuts, walnuts, pecans

1 Line several baking sheets with parchment paper.
2 Temper the chocolate (see page 18). Drop small spoonfuls of chocolate, about 2 in/5 cm in diameter, onto the prepared baking sheets. (You can also pour the chocolate into chocolate lollipop molds if you want more precisely shaped lollipops.)
3 Place some of the fruits and nuts on each chocolate round.
4 Place a lollipop stick in each round, making sure the end is fully covered by chocolate.
5 Let the mendiants set, 15 to 20 minutes, before removing from the parchment.

YIELD
Makes about 48 (2-in/5-cm) round mendiants

STORAGE
Store in an airtight container between layers of parchment paper in a cool, dry place for up to 1 week.

SWIRLED CHOCOLATE LOLLIPOPS

8 oz/225 g bittersweet chocolate

2 oz/55 g chopped nuts, nonpareils, or sprinkles

This is a surprisingly easy lollipop to make for such impressive results. This is also a fun recipe to do with kids, as they can get creative with the lollipop designs. The smaller the hole you cut in the bag for piping, the easier it is to control the flow of chocolate. If the chocolate starts spreading too much, let it cool and thicken in the bag for a bit so it keeps its shape better when piped.

1   Line several baking sheets with parchment paper. Lay out several lollipop sticks, spaced about 4 in/10 cm apart. (You can fit about four lollipops per typical-size baking sheet).

2   Temper the chocolate (see page 18). Pour the chocolate into a zipper-lock bag and snip off one corner to make a small hole about ⅛ in/4 mm wide. Pipe spirals of chocolate over each stick, making sure to cover one end of the stick so the spiral will attach.

3   Sprinkle some of the nuts or nonpareils on each chocolate spiral. Place the lollipops in the refrigerator.

4   Let the lollipops set, 15 to 20 minutes, before removing from the parchment.

YIELD

Makes about 24 small (1½-in/4-cm) lollipops

STORAGE

Store in an airtight container between layers of parchment paper in a cool, dry place for up to 1 week.

CHOCOLATE–POP ROCK LOLLIPOPS

Pop Rocks, or popping candy, has gone from Halloween treat to pastry chef's ingredient. You can find unflavored popping candy online, or you can just pick your favorite flavor from the candy aisle. The thinner the lollipops, the more the "pop" of the candy will come through.

8 oz/225 g bittersweet chocolate

¼ cup/35 g Pop Rocks or pastry rocks, plus extra for decorating

1 Lay out the lollipop molds. Place lollipop sticks in the molds.
2 Temper the chocolate (see page 18). Stir the ¼ cup Pop Rocks into the chocolate. Pour the chocolate into the molds.
3 Sprinkle additional Pop Rocks on top to decorate. Place the lollipops in the refrigerator.
4 Let the lollipops set, 15 to 20 minutes, before removing them from the molds.

YIELD

Makes about 24 small (1½-in/4-cm) round lollipops

STORAGE

Store in an airtight container between layers of parchment paper in a cool, dry place for up to 1 week.

Patience and a steady hand are all you need to make these dramatically swirled lollipops. Once you've done some simple marbling, you can try making some more complex designs. Since it's a little tricky to keep two different chocolates in temper at the same time, the chocolates in this recipe are simply melted. Just make sure to keep the lollipops in the refrigerator so they'll last longer.

MARBLED CHOCOLATE LOLLIPOPS

4 oz/110 g bittersweet chocolate

4 oz/110 g white chocolate

1 Coat the lollipop molds lightly with nonstick cooking spray. Place lollipop sticks in the molds.
2 Melt the bittersweet chocolate in a double boiler or in a metal bowl set over a saucepan of simmering water. Melt the white chocolate in a double boiler or in a metal bowl set over a saucepan of simmering water.
3 Drop small spoonfuls of dark chocolate into each mold. Drop small spoonfuls of white chocolate into each mold.
4 Use a toothpick to carefully swirl the chocolates in each mold. Place the lollipops in the refrigerator.
5 Let the lollipops set, 15 to 20 minutes, before removing them from the molds.

YIELD
Makes about 24 small (1½-in/4-cm) round lollipops

STORAGE
Store in an airtight container between layers of parchment paper in the refrigerator for up to 1 week.

This is a wonderfully sophisticated and eye-catching lollipop. White chocolate often gets overlooked in favor of dark chocolate, but here its delicate sweetness makes a perfect backdrop for the stronger raspberry and cacao nib notes.

WHITE CHOCOLATE, RASPBERRY, AND CACAO NIB LOLLIPOPS

1 Coat the lollipop molds lightly with nonstick cooking spray. Place lollipop sticks in the molds.
2 Temper the chocolate (see page 18). Stir in the orange extract. Pour the chocolate into the molds.
3 Place some of the raspberries and cacao nibs on each chocolate round. Place the lollipops in the refrigerator.
4 Let the lollipops set, 15 to 20 minutes, before removing them from the molds.

8 oz/225 g white chocolate

1 tsp orange extract

About ¼ cup/10 g freeze-dried raspberries

About ¼ cup/25 g cacao nibs

YIELD
Makes about 24 small (1½-in/4-cm) round lollipops

STORAGE
Store in an airtight container between layers of parchment paper in the refrigerator for up to 1 week.

CHOCOLATE-DIPPED MARSH-MALLOW LOLLIPOPS

You roast marshmallows on sticks over a campfire, so why not eat them off sticks as well? Although it's simple to get a bag of marshmallows and dip them in chocolate, it's worth the extra effort to make the marshmallows from scratch. Make the marshmallows the day before you want to make the lollipops. You can dip them in tempered chocolate, but this recipe offers a quick alternative. Melting chocolate and oil or shortening together will give you a smooth, sleek coating that sets to a glossy finish.

MARSHMALLOWS

1¾ cups/420 ml water

3 Tbsp unflavored gelatin

2 cups/400 g granulated sugar

1 cup/240 ml light corn syrup

1 Tbsp vanilla extract

1½ cups/150 g confectioners' sugar

1 cup/115 g potato starch or cornstarch

8 oz/225 g bittersweet chocolate

¼ cup/60 ml vegetable oil or 1 Tbsp shortening

FOR THE MARSHMALLOWS

1 Line a 9-by-13-in/23-by-33-cm baking pan with a piece of plastic wrap large enough to cover the bottom and sides and overhang the edges to act as handles. Coat the plastic wrap with nonstick cooking spray.

2 Place ¾ cup/180 ml of the water in the bowl of a stand mixer fitted with the whisk attachment. Sprinkle the gelatin evenly over the water and let dissolve and soften, 5 to 10 minutes.

3 Combine the granulated sugar, corn syrup, and remaining 1 cup/240 ml water in a large saucepan. Bring to a boil over medium-high heat.

4 Continue cooking until the mixture reaches 240°F/116°C. Remove the saucepan from the heat.

5 Turn the stand mixer to low speed and pour the sugar syrup in a slow, steady stream into the gelatin; pour down the side of the bowl to avoid having hot syrup spatter out.

6 Once all the syrup is added, turn the mixer to high speed and whip for 10 to 15 minutes, until the mixture becomes thick and glossy.

7 Add the vanilla and mix to incorporate.

CONTINUED

YIELD

Makes 24 lollipops

STORAGE

Store in an airtight container in the refrigerator for up to 1 week.

8 Pour the marshmallow into the prepared pan. Smooth out the top with a rubber spatula and let the pan sit overnight, uncovered, in a secure place at room temperature to let the marshmallow set.

9 Combine the confectioners' sugar and potato starch in a bowl. Sprinkle some of the mixture over a cutting board. Turn the marshmallow out onto the cutting board and dust the surface liberally with more of the mixture to prevent sticking.

10 Using a sharp knife or pizza cutter, cut the marshmallow into 1½-in/4-cm cubes. Toss the cubes in the confectioners' sugar mixture to coat.

11 Insert lollipop sticks into 24 of the marshmallows. (Reserve the rest for another use. You can store them in an airtight container for up to 4 weeks.)

12 Melt the chocolate in a double boiler or in a metal bowl set over a saucepan of simmering water. Stir in the vegetable oil until combined. Line a baking sheet with parchment paper.

13 Dip the marshmallows into the melted chocolate. Place on the prepared baking sheet.

14 Let the lollipops set, about 15 minutes, before removing from the parchment.

ROCKY ROAD PRETZEL LOLLIPOPS

After dipping the marshmallows in the chocolate, roll them in chopped walnuts and crushed pretzel pieces.

These lollipops are like peppermint patties on a stick. You can dip them in tempered chocolate, but this recipe offers a quick alternative. Melting chocolate and oil or shortening together will give you a smooth, sleek coating that sets to a glossy finish. It will be softer than tempered chocolate, so store the lollipops in the refrigerator and eat them quickly.

CHOCOLATE-DIPPED PEPPERMINT CREAM LOLLIPOPS

1 Combine the confectioners' sugar, cream, butter, peppermint oil, and vanilla in the bowl of a stand mixer fitted with the paddle attachment. Beat on medium speed until a smooth dough is formed.
2 Turn out the dough onto a sheet of aluminum foil. Form into a block about 4 by 4 by ½ in/10 cm by 10 cm by 12 mm.
3 Using a sharp knife, cut the dough into 1-in/2.5-cm cubes. Insert a Popsicle stick into the center of each cube.
4 Cover with plastic wrap and freeze until the cubes are solid, about 1 hour.
5 Melt the chocolate in a double boiler or metal bowl set over a saucepan of simmering water. Stir in the vegetable oil until combined. Line a baking sheet with parchment paper.
6 Dip the dough into the melted chocolate, coating completely. Place on the prepared baking sheet.
7 Let the lollipops set, about 15 minutes, before removing from the parchment.

2 cups/200 g confectioners' sugar

2 Tbsp heavy cream

1½ Tbsp unsalted butter, softened

¼ tsp peppermint oil

¼ tsp vanilla extract

8 oz/225 g bittersweet chocolate

¼ cup/60 ml vegetable oil or 1 Tbsp shortening

YIELD
Makes 16 lollipops

STORAGE
Store in an airtight container in the refrigerator for up to 1 week.

CHOCOLATE-DIPPED PEANUT BUTTER LOLLIPOPS

These lollipops are just like peanut butter cups, with a sprinkle of sea salt to make the salty-sweet contrast even better. Regular (not natural) peanut butter works best here; also, keep the cubes small, about 1½ in/4 cm, or the Popsicle sticks may not be able to support their weight.

1 cup/260 g smooth peanut butter

6 oz/170 g cream cheese, at room temperature

¾ cup/90 g confectioners' sugar

½ tsp vanilla extract

1 tsp sea salt

8 oz/225 g bittersweet chocolate

¼ cup/60 ml vegetable oil or 1 tbsp shortening

YIELD
Makes 16 lollipops

STORAGE
Store in an airtight container in the refrigerator for up to 1 week.

1 Combine the peanut butter and cream cheese in the bowl of a stand mixer fitted with the paddle attachment. Beat on medium speed until combined.

2 Add the confectioners' sugar and beat on medium speed until a smooth dough is formed. Add the vanilla and sea salt and beat to combine.

3 Turn out the dough onto a sheet of aluminum foil. Form into a block about 1½ in/4 cm thick. (If it is very soft and you are having trouble shaping it, place it in the freezer for about 30 minutes and then finish forming it.) Cover with plastic wrap and freeze until firm, about 2 hours.

4 Melt the chocolate in a double boiler or a metal bowl set over a saucepan of simmering water. Stir in the vegetable oil until combined. Line a baking sheet with parchment paper.

5 Using a sharp knife, cut the dough into 1½-in/4-cm cubes. Insert a Popsicle stick into the center of each cube.

6 Dip the dough into the melted chocolate, coating completely. Place on the prepared baking sheet.

7 Let the lollipops set, about 15 minutes, before removing from the parchment.

RESOURCES

Candy Flavor
candyflavor.com
This site sells a mind-boggling variety of both water- and oil-based flavorings.

Candyland Crafts
candylandcrafts.com
This site offers the most comprehensive selection of equipment and other tools for candy making, including molds, thermometers, flavorings, colorings, and packaging.

Fancy Flours
fancyflours.com
Fancy Flours carries silicone candy molds, which are hard to find elsewhere, as well as a great selection of decorating dusts and preprinted edible papers.

Icing Images
icingimages.com
This website specializes in edible papers. They sell preprinted papers, or you can submit your own images, and they will print custom sheets for you. They also sell edible image printers and edible inks if you want to print your own sheets at home.

Kitchen Krafts
kitchenkrafts.com
Another amazingly wide-ranging baking and candy-making site with tons of molds, tools, and packaging supplies. They carry invert sugar as well.

LorAnn Oils
lorannoils.com
LorAnn Oils makes the most commonly available flavoring oils for lollipops and other candies. They offer a huge variety of flavors and only a couple of drops are typically required to impart an intense flavor.

Molds N More
moldsnmore.com
This site specializes in molds, in nearly any shape or theme that you can imagine. They even offer to help locate a mold for you if they don't carry it.

Nature's Flavors
naturesflavors.com
Nature's Flavors offers organic and natural flavorings and colorings.

Wilton
wilton.com
Wilton offers their own line of candy-making supplies, from molds to colorings to packaging.

INDEX